SEXUAL TRAFFICKING AND MODERN-DAY SLAVERY

TERRY TEAGUE MEYER

ROSEN
PUBLISHING®

New York

Published in 2016 by The Rosen Publishing Group, Inc.
29 East 21st Street, New York, NY 10010

First Edition

Library of Congress Cataloging-in-Publication Data

Meyer, Terry Teague.
Sexual trafficking and modern-day slavery/Terry Teague Meyer.
    pages cm.—(Confronting violence against women)
Includes bibliographical references and index.
ISBN 978-1-4994-6038-4 (library bound)—
ISBN 978-1-4994-6039-1 (pbk.)—
ISBN 978-1-4994-6040-7 (6-pack)
1. Human trafficking. 2. Prostitution. 3. Human trafficking—
Prevention. I. Title.
HQ281.M49 2016
306.3'62—dc23

2014048368

Manufactured in the United States of America

CONTENTS

INTRODUCTION

Denise spent her childhood in Southern California in and out of foster care. At age thirteen, she thought she'd found love and support from an older boyfriend whom she'd met in her neighborhood. Little by little, he convinced her that she could make good money as a prostitute. Soon, this so-called boyfriend began taking the money that Denise earned having sex with other men. Denise was inarguably a victim, lured into sexual servitude by an adult male. But under the law, being forced into prostitution was no excuse. Arrested multiple times on charges of prostitution, Denise ended up in juvenile detention.

Denise's disturbing story is one among many reported on the website of the Global Freedom Center. The Global Freedom Center is one of the many organizations working today to raise awareness of the problem of human trafficking. Denise lost control over her freedom without ever leaving home. Other victims—women, children, and men—are transported across countries and continents by human traffickers. The victims are looking for a better life, but they are often forced or tricked into giving up their personal documents, their wages, and their freedom.

Slavery is not a thing of the past. According to the United Nations Children's Fund (UNICEF), an estimated twenty-seven million people around the globe are enslaved in one way or

Teenage girls may be lured into prostitution by people they trust. Runaways are often forced to resort to selling sexual services in order to survive.

another. The second annual Global Slavery Index, issued by the organization Walk Free in 2014, estimated a total of 35.8 million people enslaved in 167 countries. Such victims of forced labor and sexual exploitation are trapped by traffickers who use threats, physical and mental abuse, and even confinement to maintain control.

Modern-day slaves can be found working as domestic servants, on farms, on construction sites, and in sweatshops where clothing, electronics, or other consumer goods are manufactured. The average consumer in a developed country probably owns something made by workers under conditions of slavery. According to the organization Free the Slaves, many everyday products such as cars, computers, clothing, and even chocolate are either made by slaves or include parts or raw materials that were produced by slave labor.

Modern-day slavery is not just a problem in faraway countries where poverty is widespread. The Global Slavery Index ranked the United States as 134th out of 162 countries for prevalence of slavery. Many traffickers bring their victims to the United States, particularly through the southern border, and into big cities. Runaway children in North America, often fleeing abuse at home, are also easy victims.

For a long time, the problem of the spread of human trafficking throughout the global economy was largely ignored. Today, however, many governments, organizations, and individuals are attempting to change laws, to improve enforcement, and to rescue victims from slavery and its aftereffects.

Once freed, the victims of sexual trafficking and human slavery require special care. They may be scarred—both physically and mentally. But survivors today have reason to hope, as global attention focuses on the issue. The purpose of this resource is to raise awareness of the nature, causes, and possible cures for sexual trafficking and the many forms of modern-day slavery. Read and find resources to help free and heal victims of human trafficking, to help avoid becoming a victim yourself, and to learn how to bring an end to this form of injustice.

One World, Many Types of Victims

What is meant by the term "human trafficking?" How does it differ from historic forms of slavery? The United Nations' Protocol to Prevent, Suppress and Punish Trafficking in Persons, Especially Women and Children (2000) lists three conditions that, together, define human trafficking. The UN definition of trafficking includes: (1) an act of recruitment, transportation, transfer, or receiving persons (2) by means of force or deception for (3) the purpose of exploitation. When someone is exploited, it means that he or she is being used in an unfair or disadvantageous way that benefits another person. The UN Protocol includes as examples of exploitation forced labor, sexual exploitation, servitude, and the removal of organs.

The U.S. State Department's Trafficking in Persons (TIP) Report provides an online 101 course that helps one understand what trafficking involves. Traffickers may use trickery to get victims' consent to be transported to another area, to give up their passports, and to sign contracts that commit them to work in slave-like conditions. Traffickers also use threats to individuals and their families, physical force, or forced confinement to control victims. Trafficking does not necessarily mean that victims are moved from one place to another (although they often are). People may become victims of trafficking without ever leaving the place where they were born. In fact, some victims are even born into servitude.

Forms of Forced Labor

Kevin Bales, founder of the nongovernmental organization Free the Slaves, describes four dominant types of slavery in his book *Modern Slavery: The Secret World of 27 Million People.* Chattel slavery is most like what one thinks of as traditional slavery. A person is captured, born, or sold into permanent servitude. Today, this form of slavery is most commonly found in certain regions of Africa, particularly in regions of racial or religious conflict. Globally, chattel slavery represents only a small portion of slaves today.

UNITED STATES SLAVE TRADE.
1850.

The type of slavery once known in the United States (chattel slavery) still exists in some countries today. However, modern slavery most often involves some sort of entrapment through debts owed to traffickers.

The most common form of modern slavery is called debt bondage slavery, or bonded labor. The term "bonded labor" describes the condition in which many individuals are controlled by traffickers. Workers agree to perform labor but are indebted to those who make it possible for them to have a job. Workers are transported from one country or area to another in order to provide low-cost labor for tasks such as manufacturing, construction, or agriculture. The workers need jobs, but their situation becomes one in which they cannot benefit from their labor. Those who recruit and transport them withhold wages, supposedly until their own costs are recovered. In reality, the workers can never get free of the debt. If they receive any pay, it is not a fair wage. In addition, handlers reduce the workers' pay by deducting money for the costs of food and housing. In reality, the workers are imprisoned either economically or physically. Bonded labor does not always necessarily involve moving workers from one country or area to another. According to Bales, bondage slavery is most common in South Asia. He estimates the number of bonded labors in India alone to be around ten million.

Contract slavery, the second most common form of modern slavery, is very similar to bonded labor. Workers sign disadvantageous contracts that trap them into positions under slave-like conditions. Workers perform labor in so-called sweatshops under such contracts. The term "sweatshop" refers to a factory or workshop where manual laborers are employed at low wages working long hours under poor conditions. Unfortunately, sweatshops are all too common in the clothing industry. Women and children are particularly vulnerable to exploitation via contract slavery. The State Department's 2014 TIP Report included a picture of very young Chinese children working side by side with their parents in an unsafe factory.

In 2009, Nine Dragons Paper Holdings, a Chinese company that processes paper recycling for the city of Toronto, Canada, faced media accusations of forced labor under unsafe conditions. The company invited journalists to its factory (*shown here*) to prove that working conditions were safe.

The fourth type of modern slavery is forced labor. Forced labor may assume many forms.

In war-torn areas—particularly in Africa—children often become orphaned because of the actions of terrorists. Boys are forced to become soldiers, and girls are enslaved sexually. Sexual slavery is widespread globally as a high-profit business.

Forced labor may also be imposed by governments as well as military forces. For instance, governments may make use of prisoners for forced labor. Even those who are not imprisoned may be subject to labor with little or no compensation. For example, millions of Chinese and Cambodian citizens were forcibly removed from cities and urban centers to work in agriculture as part of Communist "reeducation programs" during the 1960s and 1970s. In his book, Kevin Bales provides the contemporary example of students in Uzbekistan who are forced to labor in cotton fields for up to three months each year.

How to Identify Signs of Trafficking

Human traffickers often transport their victims from one area or country to another. Being moved to a country with an unfamiliar language and laws makes it more difficult for victims to escape their traffickers or exercise their human rights. However, a person may be trafficked and exploited without ever leaving his or her place of birth. Indicators that someone is a victim of trafficking include loss of personal documents (such as passports, birth certificates, or other identification cards), loss of wages, and loss of freedom. Such victims may be

In times of war, children (many of them orphaned) are forced to become child soldiers or sexual slaves to invading forces.

threatened with harm to themselves or their family members. Victims may be forced to work long hours in unsafe conditions. In the case of domestic workers, a woman may be enslaved by a family and forced to work without wages or while enduring inhumane conditions, including sexual or other physical abuse.

Human smuggling is not the same as trafficking. Smuggling involves moving people from one place to another, but with the consent of the individuals. However, human smugglers often become traffickers. Smugglers may take money from those attempting to enter a country illegally and then hold them captive while demanding more money.

Tools Against Trafficking: The TVPA and the TIP

The Victims of Trafficking and Violence Protection Act (TVPA) represents the first comprehensive U.S. legislative framework that addresses the problem of human trafficking. The act was first passed in 2000 and subsequently revised and reauthorized in 2003, 2005, 2008, and 2013. The law established various tools to combat trafficking both in the United States and around the world, including:

- An interagency federal task force to combat trafficking that relies on cooperation between federal agencies and state and local law enforcement
- Services to protect and aid victims of trafficking
- Stronger legal measures to prosecute and punish traffickers
- The annual Trafficking in Persons (TIP) Report

The TIP Report is compiled by the State Department and used by the U.S. government as a diplomatic tool to engage other

U.S. secretary of state John Kerry presents the 2014 Trafficking in Persons Report to State Department staff. The report is updated each year to monitor the efforts of countries around the world to combat human trafficking.

countries in working against human trafficking. The annual report offers a global view of the nature and extent of trafficking, as well as government actions to confront the problem. The U.S. government, foreign governments, and international organizations use the TIP Report to point out where help is most needed. According to Anne Gallagher, an independent scholar and advisor to the United Nations on human trafficking, the scope of the TIP Report has expanded over the years. The first report (2001) focused mainly on sexual trafficking and covered only eighty-three countries where a "significant number" of victims were considered to be trafficked. By 2009, the report included data on 175 countries and 2 states. Furthermore, it included victims trafficked for all purposes.

COUNTING THE VICTIMS

Victims of modern slavery are not easy to find and count. Traffickers do their best to hide the exploitation of victims through the use of contracts and business terms such as "fees" and "loans" for recruitment or transportation "services." Gangs and organized crime are major players in human trafficking. They are also experts in hiding their criminal activities. Governments and legitimate businesspeople may choose to ignore the use of slave labor because it ultimately serves their purposes or profits. Most forms of modern slavery are illegal around the world, but the laws are commonly ignored or poorly enforced. The Global Slavery Index, Free the Slaves, and UNICEF each estimate the total number of victims of slavery well above twenty-five million. However, the U.S. Trafficking in Persons (TIP) Report officially identified only 46,570 victims of human trafficking in 2012. The same report listed only 7,705 prosecutions and 4,750 convictions recorded globally.

Estimates of the number of human trafficking victims vary widely depending on who is reporting and how they define "slavery." The Global Slavery Index, for example, includes forced marriage as a form of forced labor. In many cultures, very young girls may be offered in marriage in exchange for money or as repayment for debts. The young bride may be one of several wives and, in effect, act as a domestic servant and sex slave.

Efforts to estimate the vast number of enslaved individuals show progress toward ending this abuse of human rights. A report on the key achievements of the International

Labour Organization (ILO) Special Action Programme to Combat Forced Labour shows progress against trafficking between 2001 and 2011. Still, the number of victims remains in the millions.

Why Slavery Continues in the Twenty-First Century: Need and Greed

The most basic economic principals of supply and demand are at work in several ways to explain why slavery exists today. In the case of consumer goods, people in developed countries have come to expect products at low prices. Strong demand for cheap goods pressures manufacturers and retailers to keep labor costs to a minimum.

Human trafficking is big business. In May 2014, the International Labour Organization (ILO) reported that illegal profits made from the use of forced labor worldwide amounted to $150.2 billion each year. Human traffickers made roughly $21,800 each year for each victim of sexual slavery and $4,000 per victim for other types of forced labor. Human trafficking is a crime with high profits and, unfortunately, relatively little risk.

Human trafficking and slavery are huge problems worldwide because of the scope of economic and sexual inequality. People in less economically developed countries who lack sufficient food, proper housing, and clothing are easily preyed upon by traffickers. Poverty leads people to take risks in hopes of making a better life for themselves. Corruption also contributes to the problem, as law enforcement and legal officials ignore human rights abuses in exchange for bribes. Economic inequality provides traffickers with a huge labor pool of needy and vulnerable individuals.

CHAPTER 2

Sexual Trafficking

Many adults and children, regardless of sex, are exploited by human traffickers and forced to work long hours as domestic servants and in factories. Others are sexually exploited and become subject to sexually transmitted infections and abuse from both their captors and their clients. According to a fact sheet published by the human rights organization Equality Now, about two million children are exploited every year in the global commercial sex trade. Almost six in ten individuals identified as trafficking survivors had been trafficked for the purpose of sexual exploitation. While human trafficking for the purposes of sexual exploitation affects both males and females, gender inequality places a particular burden on women and girls. Because of gender inequality and the global demand for commercial sex, millions of females become entrapped in one form or another of sexual slavery.

Gender Inequality: A Global Crisis for Women and Girls

Sexual slavery disproportionately affects females. The International Labour Organization reports that 55 percent of modern slaves are women and girls and that 26 percent are under the age of eighteen. Equality Now provides the even more startling statistic that women and girls make up 98 percent of the victims of trafficking for sexual exploitation. In many cases, females are physically weaker and have less political power than males, meaning they are more easily victimized. Each year, thousands of females are kidnapped or sold to become sex workers in an "industry" where the majority of the consumers are male. The Internet has made it easier for pornographers to ensnare unsuspecting victims and to sell their wares worldwide.

With the spread of HIV and sexually transmitted infections (STIs), younger and younger girls are victimized, as those willing to pay for sex seek out virgins who do not have HIV and STIs.

Gender inequality is an important factor in the sexual enslavement of millions of women and others who identify as female. In many countries and cultures, females are not valued or protected equally by law. In some areas, elective abortions favor the birth of male children. Girls are routinely denied education equal to that of their brothers. They may also be denied equal health care and basic nutrition. Given the lack of reliable birth control in underdeveloped countries, families are often

A Yemeni former child bride, Nujud Mohammed Ali, demonstrates in support of a law to ban the marriage of girls under the age of seventeen. Child marriage of girls to much older men is a form of enslavement that is unfortunately common in some cultures.

large and resources are scarce. A family may see a daughter as little more than property to be exchanged. A young girl may be sold into a life of sexual servitude to help support other family members or simply to reduce the numbers of mouths to feed. That sexual servitude may be in the form of forced marriage as the second or third wife of a much older man. More commonly, females are trafficked in the commercial sex trade to work in a brothel, a place where customers can buy the sexual services of prostitutes.

As in the case of forced labor, girls and women are recruited through false promises. Expecting to be hired to work in offices, hotels, factories, and other legitimate businesses, they are instead forced to work in the sex trade, usually as prostitutes. Those who resist may be raped, beaten, starved, or drugged into submission. Trafficking often takes victims to countries where they are unable to speak the language and unfamiliar with their surroundings and customs. Escaping is difficult, even if victims are not physically restrained.

The sexual exploitation of women and children offers easy money and big profits to the criminals who sell the bodies and services of their victims. Criminals declare that sexual trafficking brings in more money than drugs because sexual services can be sold again and again.

As in the case of forced labor, sexual victims are lured and trafficked in a number of ways. Frequently, women are lured into sexual servitude with the promise of a legitimate job. However, children and girls in very poor countries may be sold into brothels for money. Criminals (working individually or in organizations) and predators also abduct their victims. Many women and girls are trafficked across international borders. But a staggering number of women in the United States and Canada are lured into sexual servitude in their own countries. Technology and the Internet in particular have made it easier for traffickers to take advantage of runaways and other unprotected individuals.

SEXUAL TRAFFICKING AND VIOLENCE AGAINST WOMEN AS A POLITICAL WEAPON

During times of war, rape is commonly used as a means of oppressing the opposing side. Before and during World War II, the Japanese Imperial Army seized tens of thousands of girls and women from occupied countries such as China, Korea, and the Philippines. These captives were forced to be sex slaves for the occupying armies. During the Bosnian War in the early 1990s, captured men and boys were killed

People around the world were outraged when the terrorist group Boko Haram kidnapped hundreds of schoolgirls in Nigeria. The group vowed to keep the girls in servitude or sell them as slaves to others.

(continued on the next page)

(continued from the previous page)

outright. Combatants spared the lives of women only to make them sex slaves or unwilling wives to their captors. In 2014, the radical group Boko Haram kidnapped hundreds of schoolgirls in Nigeria. The terrorist group didn't approve of education for women and used the abductions as a means of oppression and a way to make a political point. Boko Haram stated that they would use the girls as slaves or sell them to others. This horrible act sparked international outrage as people joined in support of the "Bring Back Our Girls" movement on social media.

How Technology Has Made Sexual Trafficking Easier

The Internet has made pornography readily available, and that availability has increased demand. In the past, those seeking pornography would have to visit sex shops, adult theaters, or certain newsstands. The customer might be embarrassed about being seen in such places. Now pornography of all types is available in the privacy of one's home—for a price. The demand for pornographic content and the profits that it generates have led to increased demand for subjects—especially women and minors—to be filmed and photographed. Willing adults may voluntarily work in the pornographic industry, but the depiction of minors in pornographic content is illegal. Although widely outlawed, child pornography is nevertheless common. The Federal Bureau of Investigation (FBI) reports that its task force on child pornography investigated 113 incidents in 1996. By the end of 2013, the number of cases under investigation had increased to 7,759. These figures only cover child pornography that has been reported.

The Internet has enabled sexual trafficking in several ways. For example, pornographers use the Internet to lure young victims and sell their images around the world. Digital trails can be difficult for law enforcement officers to follow in order to find these criminals and prosecute them.

In 2007, the organization Shared Hope International published the results of a twelve-month study, funded by the U.S. Department of State, surveying the market for commercial sexual exploitation in four countries: the Netherlands, Jamaica, Japan, and the United States. The report offers insight into those who are sexually exploited, those who purchase their services, and the people and organizations that bring them together. The report noted that in each of these countries, a culture of tolerance for commercial sex allowed the practice to continue and flourish. Technology is reported to be the single greatest facilitator of commercial sex in three of the countries. Only in Jamaica was word of mouth more important in connecting customers and sex workers.

Advertisements for paid sexual services were removed from the online market Craigslist in 2010 but are still available on other websites. These sites can be difficult to combat as new sites pop up as others are shut down. On many sites, commercial sex can be anonymously arranged online, and a prostitute will quickly travel to the customer's location. The pimp, or handler, can be geographically far away when the transaction takes place. This distancing of the supplier from the sexual activity makes it more difficult to prosecute the actual traffickers and easier for individuals, gangs, and criminal organizations to profit from prostitution and sexual slavery.

Child Pornography and Sex Tourism

Child prostitution and child pornography are illegal in most countries. Yet the Internet has made it much easier for pornographers to photograph, film, and distribute these images around the world. In recent years, pedophiles (individuals who are sexually attracted to children) have increasingly used the Internet to share images and to profit from child pornography. These same people may seek the actual experience of sex with young children by traveling to countries where the practice is common or poorly prosecuted (although not necessarily legal). The 2012 Shared Hope report notes that "sex tourism" involves travel by buyers of sexual services. Such travel can occur between countries or cities. Sex tourism takes sexual predators to countries where they can abuse victims in ways that are strictly outlawed and properly prosecuted in their home countries. According to the FBI, southeastern Asia is a major destination for sex tourism, and 25 percent of sex tourists to this area are Americans. Laws against child pornography and

So-called sex tourists travel to countries where laws relating to prostitution are poorly enforced. In such countries, young people are victimized by traffickers who sell sexual services. Shown here is a red light district in Pattaya, Thailand.

sex with children under the age of eighteen extend across international borders for U.S. citizens. This means that an American sex tourist can be prosecuted for his or her illegal sexual activities in another country. However, it is very difficult to capture and prosecute sexual tourists for their crimes.

Sex tourism is not only a practice of pedophiles. Major sporting events such as the FIFA World Cup and the National Football League Super Bowl attract crowds of tourists ready to party. Traffickers take advantage of such events to bring in sex workers, just as suppliers of any product increase activity to meet demand.

MYTHS and *FACTS*

MYTH Human trafficking takes place only in economically disadvantaged areas or less economically developed countries.

Victims of human trafficking come from all areas of the globe. Some victims are trafficked in their hometowns, even in middle-class and affluent areas.

MYTH Victims are at least partly to blame for their situations.

Many victims of human trafficking are physically abducted. Others may have entered willingly into what they thought was a legal or safe situation but were then cruelly deceived or abused by traffickers. Traffickers may control passports or use threats or physical violence and confinement to maintain control. No victim of sexual trafficking is to be blamed for his or her situation.

MYTH It's impossible to end modern-day slavery. The problem is too big.

Kevin Bales, cofounder of Free the Slaves, an organization working to end modern-day slavery, is optimistic that "slavery is ripe for extinction." He stresses that the effort to end slavery must take place at all levels—from local groups to international cooperation.

CHAPTER 3

The Homegrown Problem of Sexual Trafficking

Consumers of commercial sex don't necessarily have to travel the world or surf the Internet to find pornography and sexual partners. Prostitutes of all ages are readily available throughout the United States and Canada. The traffickers who supply individuals for sexual exploitation don't have to travel far, either. They find their victims close to home—often as easily as on the streets and in high schools and middle schools.

A National Epidemic

The 2007 DEMAND Report conducted by Shared Hope International stunned researchers when they found out that the majority of sex workers in the United States were not foreign nationals but American citizens, many of them minors. The report noted an estimated 14,500 to 17,500 foreigners trafficked annually into the United States, while the estimated number of U.S. citizens trafficked each year was even higher. The report estimated that one hundred thousand to three hundred thousand American children were at risk of becoming victims of commercial sexual exploitation at any time. Evidence at that time suggested that the largest number of victims were children under the age of eighteen. The report also noted that sexual exploitation of American youth was growing.

The National Human Trafficking Resource Center (NHTRC) Hotline Report gives a clear (albeit incomplete) picture of the victims of human trafficking in the United States. This annual report is based on phone calls, emails, and online contacts to the hotline. Obviously, many victims of trafficking are either unable or unwilling to seek help in this manner. The reports for 2012, 2013, and 2014 show the greatest number of contacts coming from California, Texas, Florida, and New York (in that order). The

Down Town Acupressure—which fronted as a massage parlor in Providence, Rhode Island, but was, in fact, a brothel—was eventually shut down by law enforcement. Because prostitution is illegal, sexual traffickers disguise brothels as massage parlors, health spas, and similar legal businesses.

NHTRC Hotline information reveals that trafficking pervades all areas and economic groups in the United States. The majority of the calls are from victims of sex trafficking, and the majority of the signals come from females. Citizens outnumber noncitizens by far.

Vulnerable Young People, Easy to Traffic

Child predators and sexual traffickers can easily target runaway children and teens who lack the protection afforded by a stable home and supportive family. Once they leave home, most young people lack the skills, resources, and physical strength to support themselves. Many teens quickly resort to selling their sexual services, since they have no other way to get food and shelter. The term for this is "survival sex." Traffickers, drug dealers, and petty criminals can take advantage of vulnerable young people to lure them into prostitution and drug dealing. Predators and sexual handlers trap young people into sexual slavery by offering kindness and by promising love.

Children and young people don't often run away from home without a good reason. Children of addicted, neglectful, or abusive parents may see living on the street as a better alternative to life at home. Some children are sexually victimized at home by relatives or trusted adults. The term "thrownaway" has been used to describe those children and teens who are forced out of their homes by parents who are neglectful or fail to accept their children as they are. For example, young people who admit to being sexually active or young people who identify as gay, lesbian, bisexual, or transgendered are especially at risk of being "thrown away" in this manner. Living on the streets, young people fall prey to traffickers who force them to work as strippers and prostitutes.

Even children from stable, loving families can become victims of traffickers. Natasha Falle, one founder of the Canadian support group Sextrade101, shared in a television interview how she drifted into prostitution as a teenager in the midst of her parents' divorce. Her case is typical of young people at risk for trafficking due to a lack of family support. These young people may have been abused at home or may have been in foster care. Their family life may have been severely disrupted by illness, addiction, or economic hardship. Whether they live in a country that is more economically developed or less developed, teenagers with difficult or challenging family situations are at a higher risk for human trafficking.

A family crisis or a situation of abuse or neglect may cause a teen to leave home. Once on the streets, young people risk becoming victims of traffickers and sexual predators.

Virginia Kendall and Markus Funk, both legal experts in child exploitation and trafficking, note that the rise in prosecutions against child sexual predators increased in the mid-1990s. This increase in prosecutions resulted from a better understanding of how predators lured victims. Law enforcement officers began realizing that young people were being lured to meet sexual predators in parking lots, malls, and parks. These young people had been "groomed" (or, prepared) for such meetings over periods of months. The adults picked up information online about the child's or teen's interests. The predators used this information to craft an online identity to lure the young person into a relationship. In their book *Child Exploitation and Trafficking*, Kendall and Funk tell of one such predator who assumed a number of different online identities in the course of a year in order to groom a number of potential victims at the same time.

Criminals or Victims? Specific Problems of Sexual Trafficking

Child prostitution is a crime in every state in the United States. Yet children too young to consent to sexual activity might nevertheless end up arrested for prostitution. Too often, the clients and handlers of underage prostitutes escape punishment, while these victims of sexual exploitation are arrested. The arresting officer sometimes may not be aware that the prostitute is a minor. The child may be supplied with high-quality fake identification papers to convince both the customer and law enforcement agents that he or she is an adult. Sexually trafficked children and teenagers have reason to fear punishment from their handlers. Many young people are tricked into seeing their procurers as protectors who love them. Whether out of fear or out of a sense of loyalty, young victims often refuse to help identify or testify against traffickers.

Once arrested, the young person will likely end up in juvenile detention. Detention may be the only facility readily available to place someone in order to provide protection from a trafficker. Proper facilities dedicated to housing and caring for sexually trafficked minors are almost nonexistent. These victims may be traumatized and brainwashed. They don't easily fit in at group homes or detention centers with other young people who have gotten into trouble unrelated to sexual trafficking. Child Protective Services would likely have difficulty placing them in a foster situation. These young

Juvenile victims of trafficking may be arrested for prostitution and end up in detention centers. However, some cities and organizations are working to develop programs and resources to help such young people and target their traffickers instead.

victims have special needs but few resources exist to help them. Once in the juvenile justice system, they may end up with a record that will make it even harder to escape from the criminal element.

Some members of the legal community are making efforts to recognize the problems of victims of sexual exploitation and offer positive alternatives to detention and fines. For example, a 2014 *New York Times* article reported on the tenth anniversary of the Human Trafficking Intervention Court in Queens, New York. In this court, arrested prostitutes can attend a set number of counseling sessions in exchange for having charges against them dropped. The presiding judge, Toko Serita, sees the counseling sessions as a way of putting trafficking victims in touch with the social services they need. These services can offer these victims of sexual exploitation a pathway to rehabilitation and independence. Another program called Been There Done That, operated by the Harris County Sheriff's Office in the Houston, Texas, metropolitan area, also offers prostitutes and addicts a means of escaping the cycle of exploitation.

Counseling and access to social services are essential to victims of sexual trafficking. They are often addicted to drugs and suffer from both physical and emotional abuse. Since many women become entrapped in the sex trade as teens, they also lack other important skills and training to enable them to support themselves in legitimate jobs.

10 GREAT QUESTIONS TO ASK A THERAPIST WHO WORKS WITH VICTIMS OF TRAFFICKING

1. I ran away from home to escape sexual abuse. Where can I go for help?

2. Why do I still feel love toward the person who trafficked me?

3. How can I recover from my addiction to drugs (or alcohol)?

4. How can I relate to my school peers after my experiences in the adult world?

5. My image is on the Internet. Is there any way to get back my sense of privacy?

6. How can I learn to trust people?

7. I feel like my childhood was stolen. How can I deal with that?

8. Will I be able to have a normal intimate relationship in the future?

9. How can I resume my education?

10. What will help me get past the experience of being trafficked?

CHAPTER 4

Fighting Back: Governments and Groups Against Trafficking

The United Nations and the governments of many countries around the world are actively working to end modern slavery and sexual exploitation. Nongovernmental organizations (NGOs) ranging in size and scope from local to international are aiding in this effort. Dedicated nonprofit organizations have been instrumental in pressuring governments to enact and enforce anti-trafficking measures. The issue of human trafficking relates to a number of causes such as violence against women and children and human rights. What follows is only a sample of efforts to end human trafficking. Information and links to several organizations working for change can be found at the end of this resource.

U.S. Pressure on Foreign Governments

The Victims of Trafficking and Violence Protection Act (TVPA) and the annual Trafficking in Persons (TIP) Report function in several ways to end human trafficking and aid its victims. Each year, the TIP Report classifies countries into three tiers. Tier 1 countries are countries that are in compliance with the minimum anti-trafficking standards under the TVPA. Tier 2 countries are

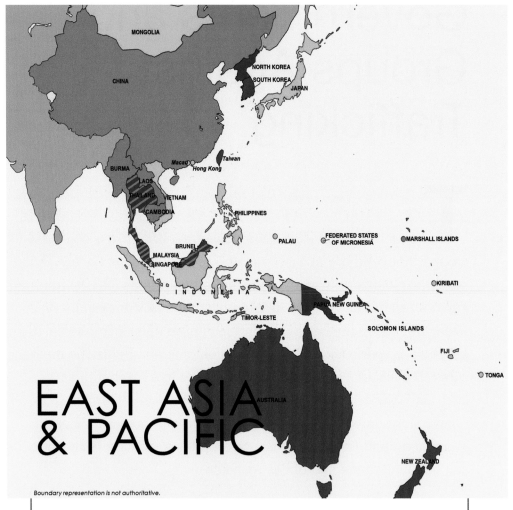

Boundary representation is not authoritative.

This map, printed in the 2014 Trafficking in Persons Report, shows the level of compliance with anti-trafficking standards under the TVPA. Tier 1 countries (shown in green) are in full compliance. Tier 2 countries (gold) are said to be making significant progress toward meeting the standards. Tier 3 countries (red) risk loss of U.S. aid due to lack of progress. Orange or red-and-orange-striped countries are on a watch list. They will be automatically downgraded to a lower tier unless they show progress within a certain amount of time.

those countries making significant efforts to come into compliance with the legislation. Countries showing no significant efforts to meet anti-trafficking goals are classed as Tier 3. Tier 3 countries may be subject to both U.S. government sanctions and loss of foreign aid.

Although the United States has been criticized for interfering in the affairs of other countries through the TVPA, the pressure has been effective. Many countries have passed laws and made serious efforts to bring an end to trafficking since trafficking reporting began. As reported in the book *Child Exploitation and Trafficking,* the government of Ecuador—classified as a Tier 2 country in 2010—passed legislation banning all forms of trafficking. The government of Ecuador also increased enforcement and prevention efforts through several public awareness campaigns. All these efforts are essential in combating trafficking. Many laws against trafficking are ineffective because of public corruption. In many countries, law enforcement officials and corrupt officials in the criminal justice system are paid off by traffickers and organized crime to look the other way. Trafficking can't be stopped unless criminals are properly prosecuted and punished.

Government Aid to Victims

The TVPA provides for substantial aid to foreign victims of trafficking who end up in the United States. The Anti-Trafficking in Persons Program (ATIP) identifies and serves victims of human trafficking by helping foreign trafficking victims become eligible for public benefits and services to the same extent as political refugees. Of course, a major problem remains, which is how to make victims aware of such services. Trafficking victims may not speak enough English to know how to look for help. Furthermore, they may be traumatized and fear that contacting the police will lead to arrest on charges of drug use, prostitution, or immigration violations.

Federal services available to victims of trafficking are administered by a number of federal agencies. Because it can be difficult to sort out where and how to get aid, the Department of Health and Human Services (HHS) has a resource guide to help social service providers aid victims. Another HHS program, the Rescue & Restore Victims of Human Trafficking campaign, is designed to make health care providers and members of the law enforcement and social service community more aware of the signs of human trafficking. In this

Individuals who fit the legal definition of a trafficking victim are entitled to a wide range of assistance and services to help them recover. For example, the government may provide them medical and mental health services, along with educational and employment assistance. Here, women train to become hairstylists.

way, these intermediaries may be more skilled in identifying victims of trafficking and getting them the help they need.

Services available to trafficking victims include cash, housing, medical, educational, and employment assistance. Medical assistance includes mental health and substance abuse services. Other resources to aid victims can be found through the Department of Justice's Office of Victims of Crime. Furthermore, California and New York have passed state-funded services to help trafficking victims. The nongovernmental organization Polaris Project monitors state laws related to trafficking and can provide updated information as state laws change.

The majority of federal benefits are not automatically available to those who claim to be trafficking victims. The Department of Health and Human Services must certify that an individual was subjected to a severe form of trafficking as defined under the TVPA. The victim must be willing to help, as much as possible, in the prosecution of the trafficker, and he or she must also obtain a special visa (known as a T Visa). Children suspected of having been trafficked are granted emergency assistance immediately. The certification process can be complicated for adults, but nongovernmental organizations can provide immediate aid to victims of trafficking. A round-the-clock resource phone number, 211, connects individuals with local community services. This service is accessible at no cost and has multilingual capabilities. This resource is funded by local governments and organizations.

The Role of Law Enforcement

Human trafficking presents a number of challenges for law enforcement and the criminal justice system. Much trafficking is conducted through complicated criminal networks crossing

Human traffickers are difficult to capture and prosecute as they work in networks across international borders. For this reason, law enforcement agencies create cooperative task forces to combat traffickers. Shown here, U.S. citizen Eric Justin Toth is arrested in Managua, Nicaragua, by FBI agents for child pornography charges.

international borders. It is much easier to identify the victims, who can be found in brothels and sweatshops, or housed in inhumane conditions. However, by the time the victims are located and freed, the traffickers who recruited and transported them are often far away. The people at the head of trafficking organizations are the most difficult to bring to justice, as they are usually far removed from the victims.

HOUSTON: ONE CITY'S PROBLEM AND SOLUTIONS

As a large port city near a major international border, the Houston, Texas, metropolitan area is a major center for human trafficking. The FBI's Houston office website includes information about the organization of anti-trafficking task forces in the area. The Human Trafficking Rescue Alliance consists of FBI agents, members of the Houston police force, the Harris County Sheriff's Office, and other local law enforcement, as well as Immigration and Customs Enforcement (ICE) agents. The Rescue Alliance focuses on locating and freeing trafficking victims. A second group including many of the same players, the Houston Innocence Lost Task Force, focuses on rescuing American children who are being sexually exploited.

Private organizations—many of them with religious affiliations—have organized to help rescued trafficking victims recover from their experiences and begin new lives. Children at Risk and Free the Captives are two Houston-based organizations. Others, such as Love146, have chapters in a number of cities.

Effective legal action against trafficking requires the efforts of a task force composed of law enforcement and criminal justice personnel. The first responder to a human trafficking case will likely be a member of a local law enforcement agency. In the case of sexual trafficking, the first responder is often a member of the vice squad. If this individual has been trained to recognize the signs of trafficking, it is more likely that the victim will get help rather than being prosecuted. A trained local officer can call on federal task force officers who have resources that may not otherwise be available. Federal authorities have the ability to serve search warrants nationwide and coordinate with other international law enforcement agencies. Agencies such as the FBI have computer forensic capabilities essential in tracking child pornography rings and in gathering evidence across borders.

Curbing Demand for Commercial Sex: Why Not Punish the Customers?

Victims of sexual trafficking become entrapped in sexual servitude because there is a big demand for their services. Laws against commercial sex are written and enforced in such a way that it is easy to arrest the prostitute—who is often a victim—and difficult to bring the trafficker to justice. For a long time, customers were not at risk of being arrested. However, today, there is a growing movement toward punishing the consumers of commercial sex in order to curb demand.

In recent years, the so-called Nordic model has shown that criminalizing the buyer has a big impact on curbing prostitution and sexual trafficking. Sweden began the movement, acknowledging that prostitution is a form of violence against women and children. In 1999, Sweden made purchasing sexual services a crime. Norway passed similar laws in 2010, and Iceland followed suit in 2011. The results of such laws show a swift and remarkable drop in sexual trafficking in these countries.

Accused of labor abuses in the 1990s, athletics giant Nike responded to public pressure. The company now works to ensure that its products are made in factories with safe and fair working conditions.

Public Pressure on the Marketplace

Raising public awareness of slave-like working conditions has proved effective in bringing about change. A May 2013 *Business Insider* article explained how public outrage against athletic-wear giant Nike caused the company to change its business model to ensure that workers making Nike products were not being treated unfairly. Articles by activist Jeff Ballinger first brought the labor abuses to light in the early 1990s. As the word spread, college students around the United States began protesting the company, causing a drop in sales. In response to public pressure and loss of sales, Nike created a Fair Labor Association to address inhumane working conditions. The company has made public the list of foreign contractors it uses and continues to audit working conditions.

In 2009, the organization United Students Against Sweatshops was successful in pressuring the clothing manufacturer Russell Athletic to rehire workers in Honduras who had been fired for forming a union. According to a November 2009 article in the *New York Times*, the student organization pressured a number of colleges and universities to suspend licensing agreements with Russell. The students also picketed the National Basketball Association finals and used social media to encourage sporting goods customers to boycott Russell products. Their efforts ultimately paid off!

CHAPTER 5

How to Help Yourself and Others

Becoming aware of the extent of human trafficking in the world makes people want to act. A basic Internet search on the topics of modern-day slavery and sexual exploitation reveals a large number of governmental and private organizations at work to combat these problems. Because of the scope of the problems, it is hard to know where to begin. For someone at risk or who has been victimized by sexual trafficking, surviving and healing is the place to start.

Avoid Becoming a Victim: Are You at Risk?

Experts agree that domestic sexual trafficking victims usually come from troubled home situations. Young people often run away to escape abuse. But leaving home only puts the young person in a very vulnerable position. He or she may end up under the control of a sexual predator or procurer. Those in an abusive or neglectful home should report the situation to a teacher, a school counselor, or an administrator. Abused children are routinely threatened not to tell others about what is going on. Often, abuse at home is directed at one child and not others. Silence only allows the abuse to continue. If you or another family member is being abused, or even if you only suspect that another family member is being abused, it's important to tell somebody who can help. State and local Child Protective Services exist just for this purpose. Child abuse in any form is against the law.

The risk of sexual exploitation might also come from a coach, an organization leader, a member of your extended family, a boyfriend or girlfriend, or a close friend. Grooming of victims begins with building trust—and then betraying it. If someone starts to ask for sexual favors or tries to become intimate against your

Sexual predators use social media to lure unsuspecting victims. Be very cautious when sharing information online. Personal information and images can quickly be spread beyond an individual's control and become very public and difficult to erase.

will, understand that the trust has already been broken. Report the behavior to another adult as soon as possible. Do not feel pressured to please a partner, friend, or anybody in your life who demands unwanted sexual activity.

Finally, be very cautious on the Internet, particularly with social media. Predators can easily hide their identities and intentions. Sharing personal information can help a predator build a fictional identity to appeal to a young person. Sexting and sharing personal images is even more dangerous, as images and films can be used as blackmail or quickly spread across the Internet. Sharing other people's personal information is also dangerous. For revenge or on a dare, teens may spread compromising pictures, rumors, and even lies about their peers. This kind of online bullying has led to suicides and ruined lives. Even if you are a minor, sharing pornographic images of an underage peer could lead to an arrest for distribution of child pornography.

If You Have Been a Victim: How to Heal

Survivors of trafficking and sexual exploitation have reason to be proud of the personal strengths that enabled them to survive. However, they more often feel weak and ashamed. It takes time to heal from such experiences, especially for a young person who is still maturing emotionally. It is important to recognize that what happened wasn't because of some personal failure or lack of character. Recovering from the effects of trafficking will take time and the help of a mental health professional. If you or someone you know has been a victim of trafficking, you understand how difficult it is to break free.

Trafficking victims are all too common, and it might be helpful to learn about the experiences of others. The 2007 film *Very Young Girls* documents the struggle of young girls in New York City trying to break free from their sexual traffickers. The girls are aided by the Girls Educational and Mentoring Services (GEMS) organization.

Rachel Lloyd, the founder of GEMS, was herself sexually exploited as a teen. She has written a memoir about her ordeal and increased the outreach of the GEMS program through the Girls Like Us campaign. Private organizations such as GEMS, Restore NYC, Houston Rescue and Restore, and the Canadian organization Sextrade101 are taking up the cause to help survivors of sexual trafficking heal and move on from their traumatic experiences.

Becoming Part of the Solution

Human trafficking in its many forms is a problem so big that it seems impossible to solve. But abolitionists such as Kevin Bales think that the world is at

Rachel Lloyd (*left*) founded the GEMS program in New York to help girls avoid or escape sexual exploitation. Lloyd counsels and supports young victims, and advocates for changes in the laws that criminalize them.

least moving in the right direction. The growing number of organizations devoted to ending trafficking shows that awareness of the problem is spreading. These organizations were founded by caring, committed individuals. Individuals like you are needed to further the cause. Here are some suggestions for how to help.

Shop Wisely

With increased awareness of the pervasive nature of human trafficking in the supply chain of goods, companies are making bold changes. The website for the organization Made in a Free World includes photos, videos, and articles that focus on the plight of trafficking victims and the efforts to improve conditions. The website reported on two successes in 2014. The technology company Hewlett-Packard (HP) in California became the first tech company to require direct employment of foreign migrant workers in its supply chain. By requiring direct employment of its foreign

As a consumer, you can help improve working conditions in foreign factories by buying from companies that support fair labor practices. The retailer H&M, for example, refuses to buy from suppliers guilty of labor abuses.

workers, HP can eliminate agents who may recruit and transport workers, only to force them to work under unfair conditions. The new policy included protection for workers' passports and other documentation. It also banned worker-paid recruitment fees. The company pledged to continue monitoring its foreign labor force to ensure that the new policies would be upheld.

The giant clothing retailer H&M also took action against slave labor by blacklisting a spinning mill in India following reports of child labor and terrible working conditions. These trends show hope for responsible manufacturing. Websites such as Slavery Footprint can give consumers information about which companies and products are likely made through slave labor. The organization Ethical Consumer includes both a list of recommended products and current boycotts (although many of these are unrelated to labor issues). Look for products that are labeled as "fair trade."

Spread the Word

UNICEF offers an online End Trafficking toolkit with many ideas to engage teachers and young people in raising awareness about the extent of modern-day slavery and the possibility of bringing about change. Free the Slaves sponsors student chapters on high school and college campuses. The Free the Slaves website includes a section titled "I Am the Change," which features individuals who are working to end modern slavery. Featured stories include those of young people in Ohio and California who have raised funds by organizing benefit concerts in their communities. Teacher Judith Meeker of Nashville, Tennessee, is helping this cause by raising local awareness about human slavery, while providing quilts to freed slaves. Through this program, American children make quilt

WATCH YOUR LANGUAGE

The language people use daily shapes how they see the world. Consider the language that you and those around you use. A "pimp" is someone who uses and abuses women. A prostitute is almost always a victim. Yet, the language of popular music and slang tends to glorify the abusers and

(continued on the next page)

Some elements of popular culture seem to approve of those who exploit and abuse women. Language is powerful and should not be used to put down women or individuals of any race or class. Here, popular rapper Snoop Dogg glamorizes the clothing and lifestyle of pimps, a profession that, in fact, capitalizes on victims of abuse and trafficking.

(continued from the previous page)

treat victims as worthless or worthy of abuse. Abolitionists who hope to end sexual trafficking object to terms such as "john" and "sex workers." They say that talking about the sex "industry" or "business" makes commercial sex seem as legitimate as any other service industry. The fact is that most people who work in this area are forced into it or forced to continue. Changing your language will help end this climate of glorification of sexual trafficking.

squares and write letters to formerly enslaved children in India who will use the quilts. Meeker is also spreading awareness through the development of lesson plans for other teachers on how to teach about modern-day slavery.

Join with Others

Gangs and organized crime are major forces in sexual enslavement. Many schools have anti-gang programs. Participating in such programs could lead to more safety in your neighborhood. The websites for national and international groups such as Free the Slaves and Human Rights Watch have information about local anti-slavery organizations for young people. Many churches participate in local rescue-and-restore efforts to help trafficking victims.

The number of trafficking victims may be staggering, but the statistics are a sign that governments and organizations are paying attention. Ending sexual trafficking and modern-day slavery is a real possibility if we continue to find and support survivors, as well as prosecute those responsible. We should all pay attention and work together to end these human rights violations.

ABDUCTION The action of forcibly taking away a person against his or her will.

BOYCOTT To refuse to buy or handle certain products as a form of protest or punishment.

BROTHEL A place of business where customers can buy the sexual services of prostitutes.

CAPITALIZE To take advantage of a situation or a person for one's own personal gain.

CHATTEL A personal possession, an item, or property other than real estate.

COERCION The use of force or threats to make someone do something against his or her will.

CONFINEMENT Keeping someone within certain limits of space and preventing him or her from leaving said limits.

DISADVANTAGED Describes a person or area in unfavorable circumstances, especially in regard to financial or social opportunities.

ENTRAPMENT The act of tricking or otherwise deceiving someone into committing a crime or engaging in a behavior that he or she would not have committed otherwise.

EXPLOITATION The use of a person or situation in an unfair or selfish way; benefitting unfairly from someone else's work.

JOHN A popular slang term for someone who buys and uses the services of a prostitute.

PERVASIVE Spread widely throughout an area or group of people, often said of an unwelcome influence or physical effect.

PIMP A man who controls prostitutes, finding clients and taking some or all of the money that they earn.

PORNOGRAPHY Also called "porn," printed or visual materials that clearly show or describe sexual acts and sexual organs for the purpose of entertainment.

PREVALENT Widespread in a particular area in a particular time.

PROCURER A person who acts as a go-between to get the services of a prostitute for another person.

PROSTITUTE A person who engages in sexual activity for payment.

SERVITUDE The state of being a slave or completely subject to another, more powerful person.

SEX TOURISM Travel for the purpose of purchasing or engaging in paid sexual services.

SOLICITATION The act of stopping someone and offering one's services or the services of another as a prostitute.

VICE SQUAD Department of a police force that enforces laws against prostitution, drugs, illegal gambling, and similar crimes.

VULNERABLE Exposed to or at risk of being attacked or harmed physically or emotionally.

Amnesty International Canada
1992 Yonge Street
Toronto, ON MSS 1Z7
Canada
(416) 363-9933
Website: http://www.anmesty.ca
Amnesty International is a worldwide organization dedicated to
    protecting and promoting human rights. The organization
    works to help individuals whose human rights have been
    violated, raise public awareness about human rights viola-
    tions, and bring about changes in laws.

Canadian Women's Foundation
133 Richmond Street West, Suite 504
Toronto, ON MSH 2L3
Canada
(866) 293-4483
Website: http://www.canadianwomen.org
The Canadian Women's Foundation is working to stop violence
    against women, improve their economic situations, and
    empower girls. It also provides support to victims of violence
    and human trafficking.

ECPAT USA
157 Montague Street
Brooklyn, NY 11201
(212) 870-2427
Website: http://www.ecpatusa.org
ECPAT is an international organization dedicated to eliminating
    the sexual trafficking and sexual exploitation of children.

Equality Now
P.O. Box 20646
Columbus Circle Station
New York, NY 10023
(212) 586-0906
Website: http://www.equalitynow.org
Equality Now advocates for the human rights of women and
    girls by increasing public awareness and promoting the
    enforcement of laws to uphold human rights.

Free the Slaves
1320 195th Street NW, Suite 600
Washington, DC 20036
(202) 775-7480
Website: http://www.freetheslaves.net
Free the Slaves is a nonprofit organization dedicated to ending
    slavery around the world. Free the Slaves works to educate
    and raise awareness among governments and the public, as
    well as to promote businesses and goods that are not made
    with slave labor.

Polaris Project
P.O. Box 65323
Washington, DC 20035
(202) 745-100l
Website: http://www.polarisproject.org
The Polaris Project helps victims of trafficking by operating
    local and national crisis hotlines. The organization conducts
    outreach to victims, works to raise awareness about traffick-
    ing, and advocates for stronger state and national
    anti-trafficking legislation.

United Nations Children's Fund (UNICEF)

UNICEF House

3 United Nations Plaza

New York, NY 10017

(212) 326-7000

Website: http://www.unicef.org

UNICEF is the world's leading advocate for children. The organization works with 190 countries to promote the protection,
education, and social inclusion of children.

Websites

Because of the changing nature of Internet links, Rosen Publishing
has developed an online list of websites related to the subject of
this book. This site is updated regularly. Please use this link to
access this list:

http://www.rosenlinks.com/CVAW/Traf

FOR FURTHER READING

Batstone, David. *Not for Sale: The Return of the Global Slave Trade—and How We Can Fight It.* New York, NY: HarperOne, 2010.

Blumen, Lorna, et al. *Girls' Respect Groups: An Innovative Program to Empower Young Women and Build Self-Esteem.* Toronto, ON: Camberley Press, 2009.

Boston Women's Health Book Collective. *Our Bodies, Ourselves.* 40th anniversary ed. New York, NY: Touchstone, 2011.

Browley, Mary Francis. *The White Umbrella: Walking with Survivors of Sex Trafficking.* Chicago, IL: Moody Publishers, 2012.

Bryfonski, Dedria, ed. *Street Teens.* Farmington Hills, MI: Greenhaven Press, 2012.

Fisher, Aaron, et al. *Silent No More: Victim 1's Fight Against Jerry Sandusky.* New York, NY: Ballantine Books, 2012.

Friedman, Mark. *Human Rights.* Chicago, IL: Heinemann Library, 2012.

Herumin, Wendy. *Child Labor Today: A Human Rights Issue.* Berkeley Heights, NJ: Enslow, 2009.

Hunter, Zach. *Be the Change: Our Guide to Freeing Slaves and Changing the World.* Grand Rapids, MI: Zondervan, 2011.

Jordheim, Alisa. *Made in the U.S.A.: The Sex Trafficking of America's Children.* Oviedo, FL: HigherLife Publishing, 2014.

Kara, Siddarth. *Sex Trafficking: Inside the Business of Modern Slavery.* New York, NY: Columbia University Press, 2010.

Klugman, Jeni, et al. *Voice and Agency: Empowering Women and Girls for Shared Prosperity.* Washington, DC: World Bank Publications, 2014.

Knight, Michelle. *Finding Me: A Decade of Darkness, a Life Reclaimed.* New York, NY: Weinstein Books, 2014.

Lloyd, Rachel. *Girls Like Us: Fighting for a World Where Girls Are Not for Sale, an Activist Finds Her Calling and Heals Herself.* New York, NY: HarperCollins, 2012.

Mam, Somaly. *The Road of Lost Innocence.* New York, NY: Spiegel & Grau, 2008.

Oselin, Sharon S. *Leaving Prostitution: Getting Out and Staying Out of Sex Work.* New York, NY: NYU Press, 2014.

Rodger, Ellen. *Human Rights Activist.* New York, NY: Crabtree Publishing, 2010.

Sher, Julian. *Somebody's Daughter: The Hidden Story of America's Prostituted Children and the Battle to Save Them.* Chicago, IL: Chicago Review Press, 2011.

Smith, Linda. *Renting Lacy: A Story of American's Prostituted Children* (A Call to Action). Vancouver, WA: Shared Hope International, 2009.

Walker, Daniel. *God in a Brothel: An Undercover Journey into Sex Trafficking and Rescue.* Downers Grove, IL: InterVarsity Press, 2011.

BIBLIOGRAPHY

Bales, Kevin, et al. *Modern Slavery: The Secret World of 27 Million People.* Oxford, England: Oneworld Publications, 2009.

Bales, Kevin, and Ron Soodalter. *The Slave Next Door: Human Trafficking and Slavery in America Today.* Berkeley, CA: University of California Press, 2009.

Bryfonski, Dedria, ed. *Human Trafficking.* Farmington Hills, MI: Greenhaven Press, 2013.

Brysk, Alison, and Austin Choi-Fitzpatrick, ed. *From Human Trafficking to Human Rights: Reframing Contemporary Slavery.* Philadelphia, PA: University of Pennsylvania Press, 2012.

Dalla, Rochelle, L., et al., ed. *Global Perspectives on Prostitution and Sex Trafficking: Africa, Asia, Middle East, and Oceania.* Plymouth, England: Lexington Books, 2011.

Equality Now. "Global Sex Trafficking Fact Sheet." Retrieved October 12, 2014 (http://www.equalitynow.org/print1010).

Federal Bureau of Investigation. "Violent Crimes Against Children." Retrieved November 19, 2014 (http://www.fbi.gov/about-us/investigate/vc_majorthefts/cac/overview-and-history).

Greenhouse, Steven. "Labor Fight Ends in Win for Students." *New York Times*, November 18, 2009. Retrieved November 12, 2014 (http://www.nytimes.com/2009/11/18/business/18labor.html?_r=1&).

Higgins, Jeff V., and Christopher M. Brady, ed. *Child Sex Trafficking in the United States.* New York, NY: Nova Science Publishers, 2012.

International Labour Office. "Marking Progress Against Child Labour: Global Estimates and Trends 2000–2012." Retrieved September 30, 2014 (http://www.ilo.org/wcmsp5/groups/

public/---ed_norm/---ipec/documents/publication/wcms
_221513.pdf).

International Labour Office. "Profits and Poverty: The
Economics of Forced Labor." Retrieved September 30, 2014
(http://www.ilo.org/wcmsp5/groups/public).

Kendall, Virginia M., and T. Markus Funk. *Child Exploitation and
Trafficking: Examining the Global Challenges and the U.S.
Responses.* Plymouth, England: Rowman and Littlefield
Publishers, 2012.

Kristof, Nicholas D., and Sheryl WuDunn. *Half the Sky: Turning
Oppression into Opportunity for Women Worldwide.* New
York, NY: Knopf, 2009.

National Human Trafficking Resource Center. "Hotline
Statistics." Retrieved October 13, 2014 (http://
traffickingresourcecenter.org/states).

Raymond, Janice G. *Not a Choice, Not a Job: Exposing the
Myths About Prostitution and the Global Sex Trade.*
Washington, DC: Potomac Books, 2013.

Shared Hope International. "DEMAND: A Comparative
Examination of Sex Tourism and Trafficking in Jamaica,
Japan, the Netherlands, and the United States." Retrieved
September 25, 2014 (http://sharedhope.org/wp-content/
uploads/2012/09/DEMAND.pdf).

UNICEF. "End Trafficking Toolkit." Retrieved September 20,
2014 (http://www.unicefusa.org/sites/default/files/End
_Trafficking_Toolkit_FINAL_0.pdf).

U.S. Department of Health and Human Services. "Services
Available to Victims of Human Trafficking: A Resource
Guide for Social Service Providers." Retrieved November
13, 2014 (https://www.acf.hhs.gov/sites/default/files/orr/
traffickingservices_0.pdf).

U.S. Department of State Office to Monitor and Combat
    Trafficking in Persons. "Trafficking in Persons Report 2014."
    Retrieved November 1, 2014 (http://www.state.gov/j/tip/rls/
    tiprpt/2014/index.htm).
Walk Free Foundation. "2014 Global Slavery Index." Retrieved
    November 28, 2014 (http://www.globalslaveryindex.org).
Watkins, Christine, ed. *Child Labor and Sweatshops.*
    Farmington Hills, MI: Greenhaven Press, 2011.

About the Author

Writer and educator Terry Teague Meyer lives in Houston, Texas. She has written several books on social issues and works for social change by volunteering as a mentor and teacher of English as a second language.

Photo Credits

Cover Alina Solovyova-Vincent/E+/Getty Images; p. 5 © iStockphoto.com/choja; p. 8 Library of Congress Prints and Photographs Division; p. 10 Imaginechina/AP Images; p. 11 Anadolu Agency/Getty Images; p. 13 Saul Loeb/AFP/Getty Images; p. 17 AFP/Getty Images; p. 19 Andrew Burton/Getty Images; p. 21 scyther5/Shutterstock.com; p. 23 Jonas Gratzer/LightRocket/Getty Images; pp. 26, 46 © AP Images; p. 28 Highwaystarz-Photography/iStock/Thinkstock; p. 30 The Washington Post/Getty Images; p. 36 © Melanie Stetson Freeman/Christian Science Monitor/The Image Works; p. 38 Oswaldo Rivas/Reuters/Landov; p. 41 pio3/Shutterstock.com; p. 44 Twin Design/Shutterstock.com; p. 47 Tupungato/Shutterstock.com; p. 49 © Warner Brothers/courtesy Everett Collection

Designer: Nicole Russo